GU00982506

ALSO BY PATRICK SÜSKIND

PATRICK SÜSKIND

Translated from the German by
ANTHEA BELL

Overlook/Rookery
New York, New York

ON LOVE AND DEATH

This edition first published in The United States of America in 2006
by The Rookery Press, Tracy Carns Ltd
in association with The Overlook Press
141 Wooster Street
New York, NY 10012
www.therookerypress.com

Original text copyright © 2005 Diogenes Verlag AG, Zürich, Switzerland
First published in the German language as *Über Liebe und Tod*
English translation copyright © 2006 Old Street Publishing

Cataloging-in-Publication Data is on file at the Library of Congress

Printed in the United States of America
FIRST EDITION

ISBN 1-58567-950-X
ISBN 13 978-1-58567-950-8

1 2 3 4 5 6 7 8 9 10

If no one asks me about it, then I know what it is; but if someone asks me about it and I try to explain it to him, then I do not know what it is.

—ST AUGUSTINE, *Confessions*

ON LOVE AND DEATH

WHAT St Augustine says of time is equally true of love. The less we think about it, the more self-evident it seems, but if we begin reflecting on the subject we find ourselves deep in trouble. This curious state of affairs is confirmed by the fact that since the beginning of cultural history man as artist, and since the time of Orpheus man as poet, has turned to few themes as persistently as to love. For poets, we are all aware, write not about what they know but about what they *don't* know, and they do so for reasons which, again, they do not know but would very much like to know in detail. This uncertainty, the poets' reiterated question, "What is love?", is the primary incentive that makes them pick up pencil, pen or lyre. (Rage, grief, exaltation, money and so on are merely secondary.) If it were not so there would be no poems, novels and plays, only factual accounts.

There seems to be some mystery inherent in love, something that we do not understand clearly and can explain only inadequately. But the same is true of the Big Bang or the question of what the weather will be like in two weeks' time. Yet the Big Bang theory and the weather forecast inspire writers and their readers far less than everything to do with love. So there must be more in it than simply its mysterious nature. Obviously all human beings assume that it is something vitally important affecting their personal lives, to such an extent that even an astrophysicist takes very little interest in the origin of the universe when he goes courting – let alone the weather.

However, could we not say the same of breathing, eating and drinking, digestion and defecation? Why, I often wondered as a child, do characters in novels never go to the bathroom? No one goes to the bathroom in fairy tales either, or in the opera, drama, films and the visual arts. One of the most important and sometimes most urgent, indeed one of the most essential of human activities has not featured in art, which instead has turned again and again, at endless length and in many variations, to the joys and sorrows, the preliminaries and all the other aspects of love which, I thought as a boy, we could perfectly well dispense with. Why has there never been a cult of excrement in human history, although cults have centered on the breasts, the vagina and the phallus? The idea may be childish but is not entirely outlandish. In Plato's *Symposium* the physician Eryximachos sees Eros at work in the filling and emptying of the body no less than in the attraction between two human souls. But Eryximachos is the most ingenuous speaker among the seven tipplers discussing the nature of love. As a natural scientist, he sees Eros as no more than a harmonizing basic principle, a kind of physical constant bringing order into the world in all imaginable areas, from agriculture to the turning of the tides, from music to an attack of hiccups. Today a man like Eryximachos would probably define love as one of the countless manifestations of the operation of enzymes, hormones or amino acids. That appears to us banal: not very edifying, and not very illuminating either. For definition is not the same as generalization; on the contrary, its purpose is to narrow down its object and mark it off from generalities. If we want to discuss love, which after all we believe is something very special, it is not much help for someone to explain that it represents a universal basic principle governing the tides and the digestive system alike. He might as well tell us that death is a thermodynamic phenomenon affecting both the amoeba and a black hole in the constellation of Pegasus – and he would still have told us nothing.

It may be that love too has its physical, mechanical and vegetative aspects – Stendhal calls it a crystallization, and in another passage a fever; being in love is a frenzy, says Socrates in the *Phaedros*, a sickness, a madness. But not a harmful frenzy, he adds, the finest frenzy there is; and not a harmful illness, or a truly human madness in the pathological sense, but a *mania* inspired by and yearning for the divine, a god-like madness, lending wings to the earthbound soul. It is true, he says, that Eros himself is not a god, is neither good nor bad, neither beautiful nor ugly, but a great daemon, a mediator between mankind and the gods, a force instilling in human beings a desire for what they lack: beauty, virtue, happiness, perfection – all of them divine attributes whose reflection the lover sees in the beloved – and finally even immortality. Eros is "witness to the urgency of love to procreate and bring forth in beauty," says Diotima, the "wisest of women," of whom Socrates speaks in the *Symposium*. And this "procreation and bringing forth," both in the physical and animal sense, but even more in its intellectual, didactic, artistic, political and philosophical aspects, in short all that we call creativity, is mankind's share in immortality, since it continues to work on beyond his death and to exist. "In beauty" is a not unimportant addition: to conceive and bear *in beauty* is to do so in the longing for those divine attributes that elude us as human beings.

This is strong stuff, and has not lost its power in the last two and a half millennia. From slushy pop songs to *Fidelio* and *Die Zauberflöte*, from cheap novels to Kleist's *Amphitryon*, writers and musicians are trying to give expression in their works to the belief that love is sublime, heavenly, redeeming, and the terminology in which they write and sing of it has remained religious to this day – in which it may be seen as sufficiently far from excrement.

Three Examples

NOT LONG AGO I WAS DRIVING THROUGH TOWN. At a junction notorious for its short green lights I had to wait some time in one of the four or five rows of vehicles moving a little way forward only every few minutes. To left and right of me drivers were lighting cigarettes, fiddling with their radios, glancing at the newspaper, or if they were women freshening their make-up. The kind of thing you do when you are stuck in a small traffic jam.

In the car directly in front of me, however, a large and elderly Opel the color of milky coffee, its trunk bearing stickers of the silliest kind ("Honk if you're horny"), a young couple had their own way of passing the time; they kept putting their heads close together to stare at each other with enraptured smiles, to talk to, finger, kiss and lick one another. They moved apart only for brief moments, as if startled, turned their suddenly blank faces to look out of their respective side windows, only to come together again a couple of seconds later with a sudden movement, as if they hadn't seen one another for months, before they went on kissing, gazing at one another as if each saw a miracle. She was at the wheel, a girl of the little mouse type, pretty profile, very smooth neck, a great deal of curly hair that shook slightly as she laughed, small white teeth, lively eyes. He, on the other hand, lounging rather than sitting in the passenger seat, right foot hanging out of the window, left arm draped around her shoulders in a lordly manner, was the kind of young man you really wouldn't want to know. A gruesome sight, all his movements ungainly, fat neck, shaven skull, silver ring in his left ear, pimply skin, snub nose, and his mouth always half open; he didn't remove his chewing gum even to kiss her. Any objective observer could only think that the sweet girl really deserved something better than this ghastly lout.

She herself didn't seem to think so at all. She interrupted their dalliance only briefly to move forward next time the lights turned green. Then she once again had eyes for him alone, resumed their lovey-dovey game, moved close to kiss him and let him nudge her. Even worse, she reached for his right hand and took his sausage fingers one by one between her spotless teeth, nibbling and licking them, while he plunged his large left paw into the glory of her brown hair to fumble around in it, probably also exerting pressure until, in response to the pressure of his hand or her own desires – who knows? – she lowered her head and disappeared from my sight, dropping sideways to his lap where she went on working on him, to which the lout responded by flinging back his head and grotesquely waggling the leg that hung out of the window with a dirty running shoe on its foot.

Meanwhile the lights had turned green again, and drivers behind me were beginning to honk their car horns. At last the girl surfaced, tousled and radiant, sat up in her seat, and in response to more honking the young man swung round, turned his vulgar, gum-chewing visage in my direction (though I had not in fact been honking), and made the most obscene gesture in the world with the finger that had just been groping her beautiful hair. She stepped on the gas and shot away, tires squealing, just before the lights turned red and forced me and the rest of the line of cars to stop.

"Mann und Weib und Weib und Mann reichen an die Gottheit an," runs the duet in *Die Zauberflöte.* Man and woman, woman and man together approach

divinity. This hymn to love is sung by Pamina and Papageno. At the end of the opera, and thanks to Eros, Pamina will enter the temple of wisdom with her lover Tamino. Meanwhile Papageno, whose ambitions are earthier and who hopes at most for a little "entertaining company" from his beloved Papagena as well as the physical delights of love, will still partake of divine happiness and immortality through their many small children. Both kinds of love are beautiful and good and whole, in the Platonic sense. But how – so I wondered as I waited at the red lights and watched the young couple race across the junction – how would Eros contrive to make *those two* procreate and bring forth *in beauty*?

Well, I told myself, they're still young, very young, not yet twenty and thus erotically stupid. *He*, at least, is stupidity personified. But even she, the pretty little girl, is foolish, as unfortunately pretty little girls sometimes are. And according to

Plato, fools do not strive for the beautiful and the good, for divine bliss, because they are satisfied with themselves. The wise do not strive for it either because they already have those things. Only the people in between, half-way between fools and the wise, you and I and all the others waiting patiently here in a traffic jam for the next green light, are vulnerable to the arrow of Eros. And the scene just played out in the milky-coffee-colored Opel, I told myself, has nothing to do with love, or anything even remotely connected with it, but with a distasteful futility.

A FEW DAYS LATER I WAS INVITED TO A DINNER of some size in a well-to-do household. On such occasions there is usually a guest of honor for whose sake the other guests are there, to have the opportunity of meeting him or her, which is all very pleasant and praiseworthy. In this case the guests of honor were a newly married couple: she a well-known patron of the arts about seventy years old, blonde and plump; he in his early fifties, a Romanian choreographer and former dancer with pitch-black hair and an admirably straight backbone. The gossip columns of the papers had already printed stories about both of them, usually writing derisively about her money and his career, her former husbands (5) and his former wives (3), and the age difference between them (17 years). But anyone seeing them in the flesh was instantly convinced that Eros, rather than any social or financial calculations, must have played the leading part in the union of this unusual couple. Not only were they unable to take their eyes off one another all evening, they couldn't keep their hands to themselves either. They clung as close as two young monkeys, they seemed to be as inextricably intertwined as Philemon and Baucis. They did not shake hands with the other guests as they arrived, because each was holding both the other's hands. Sitting on the veranda for an aperitif, they shared the same basket chair, drank orange juice from the same glass, and nibbled at one and the same breadstick. It was impossible to talk to either of them because they were talking, or rather whispering, only to each other, in an amorous hotchpotch of French, Spanish and German that was incomprehensible to outsiders. When we went to sit down at the table a restlessness came over them; they fluttered up to the mistress of the house in some agitation and asked for a change in the seating plan, which had been intended to separate all the couples invited. She complied with their request, and let them sit next to each other. They moved their chairs so close that they were able to eat side by side as if sitting on a small bench, she using her right hand and he his left hand, for they needed their other hands to keep touching and holding one another. They looked sad when they inevitably had to take their eyes off each other for a moment or so to attend to their plates:

two separate plates from which each must eat alone, when they would much rather have eaten from a single plate – if at all, for they ate very little. Eating obviously seemed to them a painful waste of time, an unnecessary distraction which prevented them from basking in each other's gaze and looking their fill at one another. Even before the dessert course they asked for a taxi, and then rose at once from the table, nodded briefly to the company in a collective farewell and floated away, merging together as one. They left the other guests behind in a state of bafflement and probably relief.

Is *that* true love? A kind of frenzy, certainly. A madness, no doubt. But the finest frenzy there is? A delusion inspired by the divine and leading to the divine? It is hard to think so.

I N THE SUMMER OF 1950 A MAN OF SEVENTY-five is spending three weeks at the Grand Hotel

Dolder in Zürich with his wife and his eldest daughter. He has been married for forty-five years, has fathered six children, and is a world-famous writer. His birthday was celebrated a few days earlier with great ceremony and public participation; he has speeches to make, essays to write, an enormous correspondence to deal with, a novel to finish, guests to see, interviews to give. He is anxious about international politics, the Korean war that is just breaking out, the increasingly problematic situation in the United States where he lives in exile; his wife is about to have a rather dangerous operation; his daughter takes morphine for her gall bladder disorders. He himself is constantly plagued by minor complaints, from otitis to insomnia. In short, the man is troubled by more than enough problems and anxieties, and certainly has no intention of embarking on an erotic escapade – at his age, too.

One afternoon, however, taking tea in the

hotel garden, he is served by an assistant waiter aged nineteen with wavy brown hair, brown eyes, fine hands, a plump neck, and a face "not worthy of celebration" in profile, but "infinitely engaging" seen full on. The young man's name is Franzl, he is the son of a Tegernsee innkeeper, he is training at the Dolder and will end his career forty years later as a head waiter at grand banquets in New York. Not even in his dreams does he guess what perturbation his figure, his eyes, and his "soft, gentle" voice with its slight Bavarian accent will cause the old writer, who is overwhelmed. "So here it is once more," he writes in his diary, "here is love again, that sense of captivation by another human being, that deep longing – it hasn't happened for twenty-five years, yet it was to come to me again." His own world-wide fame suddenly seems to matter little to him, his concern for his sick wife retreats into the background, international politics and the Korean war no longer matter. But the question of whether the Italian head waiter or Franzl serves the tomato soup at dinner is of supreme importance. He will be a happy man if he can exchange a few words with Franzl, ask him for a light for his cigarette, or tip him five francs "for serving at table so nicely yesterday," and be rewarded with a friendly smile. No more than that happens between the two of them, but from morning until night and even in his dreams, the writer's thoughts circle around his "darling" whom he also, and very much in Plato's sense, calls the one who "arouses" and "enchants" him. He wakes in the middle of the night feeling, as he notes with both pride and shame, a "strong sense of empowerment and release." He becomes increasingly nervous, less able to concentrate and work, sleeps even worse than usual, has to take valerian and read Adorno "as a sedative," which does not help, for he feels that everything is "permeated and overshadowed […] by grief for want of the one who arouses me, by pain, love, nervous expectation, hours of reverie, distraction of mind and suffering."

Meanwhile his wife is better and they leave the Hotel Dolder to spend a few more weeks of rest and relaxation in the Engadine. But the arrow of Eros has gone deep, and the old man cannot forget the young waiter. The pain he feels for him has "deepened and strengthened into a general mourning for my life and my love," he writes in his diary, and he is "close to wishing to die, because I can no longer endure my longing for the divine boy." He tries to distract his mind by watching another young man from the window of his hotel room, a tennis player whose "Hermes-like legs" he admires – it is no good. He waits desperately for a letter from the assistant waiter Franzl. He had written to him, on the pretext that he might perhaps be able to help him in his career, leaving his address. When the letter from Franzl finally arrives – an expression of thanks, very plain and conventional,

containing "small grammatical errors," and culmi-
nating in the sentence "I was really very pleased
that you thought of me," which could hardly be
surpassed for banality – the world-famous writer,
regarded as one of the greatest stylists in the German
language, is deeply moved and happy. The letter
gives him "enduring joy," he will keep it like a holy
relic, that sentence "I was really very pleased . . ."
in particular enraptures him. Months later, long after
he is back in America, he will still be delighted by
it, and to the end of his life he will not forget the
boy who wrote to him without ulterior motive or
any idea of his feelings. "He is accepted into the
gallery," he notes, meaning: into his imaginary
pantheon, in which there are four more young
men to whom he has owed the central amorous
experiences of his life, and to all of whom, in one
way or another, he has set up a memorial in and
through his work.

The waiter too will have such a memorial, or

rather, he will arouse the writer artistically in his last work. He remains the one who arouses him sexually to the end. A year later the old man realizes, sadly, that he is no longer capable of full masturbation, and thus his sexual life is at an end. He dreams once more of his lover, and takes his leave of him in that dream with a kiss, the kiss he never dared to give in real life and never received.

THESE THREE EXAMPLES OF LOVE AND INFATUA-tion illustrate Plato's analysis in very different ways. He would probably have relegated the conduct of the young people in the Opel Omega to the category of animal love, whose place of worship is at best the house of the hetaerae but could never be the temple of Aphrodite. With the odd couple invited to that dinner as guests of honor, one might fear that Eros went no further than delusion. The writer's love for the under-waiter, on the other hand, fulfills the criteria of what Eros is in several respects. It is frenzied, it sees – and names – the divine in the beauty of the beloved, it ultimately urges the lover towards creativity, and it seeks and finds immortality, in this case in the writer's work. And yet we feel that this is not the right way either. If we think of what we understand by the term "love," however vague and indefinite our idea of it may be, something essential is missing. It is not because of the homoerotic element in this case – if the writer's preferences had been different Franzl might just as well have been a Franziska (and with Goethe in his old age it was an Ulrike). No, the difficulty is in the fact that this love is entirely one-sided, and the writer deliberately refrains from even attempting to make it mutual. For he knows very well that then – whether or not the attempt suc-ceeds – it will very quickly turn out to be a mere tri-fle, an empty void (Franzl is no Alcibiades), and, more important, will be of no use to what is really all that he deeply cares about: himself and his work. Much as the old man suffers from the impossibility of realizing his love, he quickly and deliberately determines to make an instrument of it, whether through manual narcissism or in sublimation. We almost suspect that he exposed himself to erotic temptations throughout his life because only despairing rejection of them could inspire his true passions.

Of course there is nothing at all wrong with that, particularly not in a writer to whom we owe the most moving prose works in German ever written on the theme of Eros. But just as we may not necessarily be well advised to go to a conjuror to learn how to catch a white rabbit, even though he can bring one out of a hat with such aplomb, the story of the writer and the waiter is not the best place to learn about love.

However, there is something else we can conclude from their story and from the other two examples: a considerable amount of stupidity is evident in love and infatuation. I would recommend reading one's own love letters twenty or thirty years after writing them. A blush of shame rises in the face of such bleak documentation of foolishness, arrogance, impertinence and blindness. The content is banal, the style embarrassing. One can hardly understand how even a person of no more than average intellect was ever capable of feeling, thinking and writing such nonsense. To be sure, in a kindly mood one might call it childish, pitiful, even touching. And yet it seems more appropriate to describe it as a temporary loss of intelligence induced by love. We all know how impossible it is to hold a rational conversation with a lover, least of all about the object of his love. The best-meant warnings, irrefutable arguments and obviously true comments come up against a huge but – "*But* I love her (or him)!" – or, even worse, are regarded as hostile acts inspired by envy, and treated as such. It is not uncommon for friendships of many years' duration and established relationships to be broken in this way. The lover doesn't mind. He is ready to give up anything but his adoration of the beloved, to which everything around him must at all costs be subordinated. One look at the look of a lover looking at his beloved is enough to show that the lover's eyes are empty; he has surrendered himself entirely. All the wit, brains, shrewdness, curiosity and caution he once had have disappeared. What is left – as in the glance of the man transfigured thinking that he sees God – is an expression of the purest folly. In fact this phenomenon of idiocy caused by love is by no means confined to the sexual variety. It is found just as often in the doglike devotion of parents to children who have turned out badly, or the spiritual love of nuns for their heavenly spouse – not to mention the worship of subjects for the Fatherland or their beloved Führer. The price paid for love is always the loss of reason, abandonment of the self, and thus the surrender of adult responsibility. The result in harmless cases is that lovers look ridiculous, in the worst case it can be political disaster on a world scale.

If the love is reciprocated, and we are dealing with a loving couple, the consequences for their immediate environment and the wider context may not be so dangerous, since the partners will largely neutralize their own folly, but in human and ethical terms they are nothing short of lamentable. Enamored couples are frequently inclined to indulge in a form of social autism (think of that couple at dinner) – or social arrogance (as with the young people in the car). In both cases they are lost to the world, whether because they are so absorbed in each other and self-sufficient that they forget everything around them, or because in the elation they feel as a unique pair they scorn the world, regarding those who are not in the clutches of the sacred madness of Eros as fools and showing them the door.

All this is curious and intriguing, since love is regarded as the best and most beautiful thing that a human being can give and experience, and since it is supposed to make us capable of the greatest and highest that we can achieve. How do we solve this conundrum? How can what stultifies and potentially brutalizes us be felt and described as the highest happiness? Is love only a sickness after all, and not the most beautiful but the most terrible of sicknesses? Or is it a poison, and the dosage decides whether its effect is beneficial or devastating? Help, Socrates, help!

The soul of man, says Socrates, is not homogeneous, but has three parts, and he compares it to a team which we have to picture as a fighting chariot of the ancient world, with two horses and a charioteer. It is an art to keep such a vehicle on the road anyway, but it becomes a breakneck adventure if, as with the team of the soul, only one of the horses is naturally noble, quick to learn and docile, while the other is ill-natured, wild and unruly. When Eros enters the equation too, when the tripartite soul begins to love and catches sight of the beloved, the ill-matched team runs completely out of control. The bad horse races away like a berserker, has to be whipped frequently and forcibly restrained, leaving its sides sore and its mouth bleeding, until in the end it humbly obeys the charioteer and, like the good horse, hesitantly and modestly approaches the beloved. Once the beloved is wooed and won he or she, feeling love in return, will allow touching and kissing, and will finally sink down on a bed. And only now, so says Socrates and so writes Plato, "as they lie together, the unruly horse of the lover has something to say to the charioteer on the shared bed, and demands a little enjoyment in return for his many troubles."

By the way: according to Plato, the soul is

immortal. And he does mean every soul. Even the soul in which the charioteer is weak and the bad horse is in charge. But Eros does not lend wings to that soul, or to those souls who believe they can do without Eros either. After death they all go to dungeons underground to do penance for a thousand years. The others, however – and it seems that there cannot be many of them, souls whose charioteers are strong and thoughtful enough not to give the bad horse free rein, yet do not avoid love but seek it and look it in the eye – these are given wings by Eros after death, and they rise and fly in the light, approaching the sphere where the gods dwell.

A beautiful parable. But a parable that quite unexpectedly leads us from the subject of love to the subject of death.

DEATH AS A SUBJECT? IS NOT DEATH THE NON-subject *par excellence*? However cheerfully we may chatter about love, there is little to say about death. It leaves us speechless. Once, we are told, in the good old days, in ancient times it was different, Death was more loquacious and affable, was part of society and the family, encounters with him were not avoided, and if he was not a close friend at least he was on familiar terms with mankind. There has been a fundamental change over the last two hundred years. Death has fallen silent and commands our silence, and we are happy to comply; indeed, we preserve a deathly hush. And not because we know nothing about it – that, as everyone knows, is no reason at all to keep one's mouth shut – no, it is simply because death is the spirit of the eternal negative, a spoilsport, literally a killjoy, and we want nothing to do with such characters today.

So how can this aloof and dislikeable figure be linked with Eros, who is more inclined to cheerfulness and lust, and not as his opposite – which would at least look consistent – but as his companion? And how can the initiative behind this companionship come not from Thanatos (the boor-ish creature is much too lazy and self-satisfied for that), but from Eros himself, the one who "arouses," who "enchants," who is allegedly the source of every creative impulse?

In Oscar Wilde's story the beautiful Princess Salomé falls in love with a religious fanatic who is too cowardly even to look at her, but blind and brave enough to risk death by rejecting her, whereupon she has his head cut off, blissfully kisses his dead lips as they drip blood, and informs us that the mystery of love is greater than the mystery of death. "So who is Salomé?" we may object. "A spoiled girl of twelve or fourteen who knows little about love and nothing at all about death." Yet even the old writer in our third example, who knew a great deal about both and was exceptionally clever, associates love with death, cer-tainly in his work, but also in his life. In the midst of his infatuation he says, as quoted above, that he is "close to wishing to die." "Farewell forever, charming boy!" he writes in his diary. "I will live a little longer, do a little more, and die. And you too will mature as you go on through life, and will die some day. O incomprehensible life that affirms itself in love." But it is not only, as here, in moments of farewell and renunciation, moments of the *pain* of love that Thanatos comes together with Eros; in the opinion of Stendhal – who must be described as an expert on this subject in spite of his over-heated and confused nature – love in general is on easy terms with death. "True love," he writes, "makes thoughts of death frequent, easy, and not terrifying; it becomes a simple object of comparison, the price one is ready to pay for much."

We understand this. We understand both attitudes: the one seeking death as the only possible liberation from the unbearable pain of love, and the other, as it were chivalrous attitude, accepting death as a necessary risk taken in pursuit of the erotic quarry, particularly at times and in societies where swords and pistols were swiftly drawn. Neither can be described as exemplary and worthy of imitation, both may be regarded as a deplorable aberration of the erotic drive, to be ascribed to its frenzied and indeed pathological nature, but as I said above, we can understand such things, that is to say, we can put ourselves in the place of human beings who kill themselves or die for love. If it were not so, how could we read *Werther, Anna Karenina, Madame Bovary* or *Effi Briest* unmoved? Yet the point where empathy and understanding end and interest wanes, giving way to outright repugnance, is reached when Eros throws himself violently into the arms of Thanatos as if to merge with him, when love seeks to find its highest and purest form, indeed its fulfillment, in death.

This unfortunate liaison – as we learn from Philippe Ariès's *The Hour of our Death* – began as early as the beginning of the sixteenth century. At this date the visual arts first turn the medieval, dark but chaste *danse macabre* into a lascivious *danse érotique.* Later the phenomenon takes on necrophiliac features, followed by sadistic aspects even before de Sade, and makes its way into literature. The myth of the hanged man's erection, which is pure nonsense, is invented; the French language introduces the term *la petite mort* as a synonym for orgasm, an expression which at first glance seems striking and pretty (and was probably originally meant ironically), but at second glance appears wholly inappropriate. Finally, in the nineteenth century that brings so much to over-ripeness, the love of death and love in death culminate in ecstasy: Novalis's *Hymns to Night* are nothing but enraptured love poems addressed to death, and at the other end of the Romantic period Baudelaire's *Fleurs du Mal,* mingling the realistic and the Baroque, spread their sharp and venereal smell of decomposition. "He inhales the smell of corpses like an aphrodisiac perfume," Anatole France wrote of him.

Kleist is positively bursting with the joys of life and erotic excitement in his last letters, when he has his sights trained on suicide. He has been looking for months for a woman who would be ready to die with him. At last he has found one sick and depressive and stupid enough to take the part with enthusiasm, the wife of a minor civil servant – one hardly likes to think how mediocre, joyless, frigid and full of religious delusion a life like hers had been if she hoped to find its climactic moment in being shot! She writes him spellbound little notes, he writes her love letters that hardly have their equal for beauty in the German language. He kneels down morning and evening to "thank God for a life more full of torment" than any man ever led, because "He repays me with the most sublime and sensual of all deaths." To his cousin, who had been his confidante until now, he writes a kind of letter of apology a week before his planned death, asking her to understand that he has found another woman – the civil servant's wife – whom he loves more: "Will it console you if I say that I would never have preferred this friend to you if she had wanted only to live with me?" But unfortunately his cousin has several times rejected his suggestion that they die together, whereas the other "idolized friend" was ready to agree at once, and "I cannot tell you with what inexpressible, irresistible force that consent drew me to her breast." A torrent of bliss such as he has never felt before, he says, is sweeping him away, "and I cannot deny," he concludes, "that her grave is dearer to me than the beds of all the empresses in the world." He does not omit to add a brief salutation in which he tells his "dear friend," meaning his cousin, that he hopes God will soon call her too "to that better world, where all of us, with the love of angels, will be able to press each other to our hearts. – Adieu."

Goethe has been criticized for remarking that

Kleist – whose genius, incidentally, he did not fail to recognize – had always filled him with a sense of "terror and abhorrence." One might well agree, "What else?" and add that the word abhorrence in its original sense is not derogatory but implies an instinctive flinching, a "shuddering away," to keep something far from one's own nature – a very understandable attitude, particularly if one's own nature may itself not be entirely impervious to the terrible and abhorrent. Certainly Werther's suicide falls into a different category from Kleist's. Werther kills himself or "sacrifices himself" for the beloved, he says, because a life with her is denied him – or so at least he believes. Kleist, on the other hand, was fascinated all his life by suicide, saw suicide pacts as an expression of the utmost intimacy and mutual fidelity, and finally he commits suicide in company because he expects the experience to give him what we would describe as the ultimate erotic kick. Yet there are similarities between Werther's

47

(fictional) farewell letters to Lotte and Kleist's last letters to his cousin and sister, which of course are not just prose communications but literature on the highest level. Similarly the entire act, in its perfect planning and staging, in its literary documentation and calculated effect on the public, has something terribly well-constructed about it, and indeed – *sit venia verbo* – can be described as Kleist's magnum opus.

Werther does confess that "the angry thought" crept into his heart of killing Lotte's husband Albert or even Lotte herself instead of committing suicide, for "one of us three must be gone." He does not suggest that Lotte and he go to their deaths together, but dies claiming that his death makes her his forever, he is only going ahead and will wait in another world until she comes. And then, he writes to her, "I will fly to you, and hold you, and be with you in eternal embraces before the face of infinity." It is not so very far from here to Kleist's erotic suicide.

The older Goethe did not like to be reminded of such things. Although *The Sorrows of Young Werther* had once been the cornerstone of his fame, he declared the work something that he had now left behind, and called the young enthusiasts who did themselves violence in imitation of Werther idiots, weak natures who deserved nothing better than such a foolish death. No wonder, then, that he was disturbed by Kleist, who was anything but a weakling, and there is something suspect in the way he was soon dismissing not just the man himself but his entire work as barbaric nonsense, for the temptations to which Kleist was exposed, and to which at last he surrendered without inhibition, were far from alien to Goethe.

Many years later – by now Kleist is long buried – Goethe writes one of his most famous poems, published in a ladies' almanac as *Vollendung* [Perfection] and then as *Selige Sehnsucht* [Blissful Yearning] in the *West-Eastern Divan:* five cross-rhyming quatrains, the two opening lines briefly indicating that what follows is not for everyone, only for a few of the wise.

> Tell it only to the wise,
> For this thought the crowd will spurn:

Then he goes straight to the point with a hollow drumbeat:

> Those living souls I chiefly prize
> Who for fiery death do yearn.

And he makes an image that has fascinated him all his life into a metaphor, the image of the moth plunging to its death, irresistibly drawn to the naked flame. He sets this metaphor against a dark, familiar background, a painting with highly erotic associations –

In the cool of nights of love
Engendering as you were engendered,
That strange sensation from above
By candlelight comes many-splendored.

Midst the shadows you no longer
Waiting in their darkness tarry.
New desires, ever stronger,
You to higher mating carry.

Distance could not bar your flight,
Spellbound on swift wings you came,
At last to fly, desiring light,
As the moth into the flame.

– only to proclaim in the last verse, which despite
the author's warning in the opening lines became so
popular that it was much anthologized:

And until that final death,

Transfiguring, takes you to its breast,
On this dark earth you but draw breath
Lingering here, a somber guest.

Goethe was extremely reticent over the publication of certain poems, and preferred to lock them away in a drawer like private treasures, bringing them out only to show them to the favored few. It is a remarkable fact that many of the Venetian sonnets, Roman elegies, the poem *Das Tagebuch* [The Diary] and similar erotica had to stay in that drawer, while the lyric just quoted was allowed to appear in a demure ladies' almanac, for this is by far the most scandalous of these works, and its author is in no way less radical than Kleist, whom he described as barbaric. It is true that whereas Kleist embarks on his headlong descent without ambiguity and never deviating from his single track, Goethe, in appearing to tone down the subject, could be said to allow escape routes into potential interpretations: religious, meta-morphological, epistemological. And where Kleist's manner is shrill, exacerbated and over-excited, Goethe lulls us with his wealth of verbal melody and his air of the serene wisdom of old age, thus diverting us from the terrible object of fascination that occupies his mind as it did Kleist's: an erotic longing for death.

Richard Wagner was less bashful about it. In *Tristan und Isolde* neither the melodic richness of the music nor the libretto and the action cast a veil over that terrible *mésalliance.* Twilight reigns even in the first bar of the overture. In the first act a deadly potion is offered and turns out to be a love philtre; in the second, the night of love turns out to be an hour of dedication to the "longing for death in love" – the *Liebestod* – but not discreetly, as in Goethe's "strange sensation" felt by candlelight, but with jubilation, rejoicing and triumph – very much in the spirit of Kleist although, as befits an opera, in much simpler language. And in the last act all is at stake: at the moment when Isolde, whom Tristan desires so much, comes back to him, could heal him and *live* with him, he tears the bandages from his wound in order to stagger towards her, bleeding to death and dying in her arms. She is only briefly irritated by his failure to pay proper attention to the timing and arrive too soon; then "she gazes at Tristan's body with increasing rapture" and delivers the longest orgasm in musical history (about seven and a half minutes) before falling dead in his arms in her own turn.

Kleist took less time about it on 21 November 1811, on a height by the banks of the Kleiner Wannsee near Potsdam. A waitress at the nearby inn told the police who questioned her that she had taken "fifty paces" after hearing the first shot, and was still thinking, "Those strangers! Fooling about with a gun!" when she heard the second. That means that there must have been less than a minute between them. He needed that time to make sure that his companion – one hesitates to write "his lover" – was really dead after he had shot her in the heart, the shot passing through her ribs below her left breast, then perhaps to lay her down (she was found lying on her back with a contented smile on her face), throw away the pistol he had just fired, pick up a freshly loaded one (he had brought three with him to be on the safe side), kneel down between the woman's feet, and then fire the bullet through his mouth and into his brain.

O RPHEUS STANDS AT THE BEGINNING OF THE history of those who, for the sake of love, refuse to accept death. There were others who, while still alive, ventured to steal a glance at the shadow world of Hades, or take a step into it, but none who, like Orpheus, entered the realm of the dead to bring his beloved back to life. The name of Orpheus stands for a wealth of other achievements and brilliant actions, as well as this not entirely successful bravura performance. He is the forefather of lyric song, the art of words and music; his singing was so extraordinarily beautiful that he captivated and calmed not only human beings but also animals, plants, even inanimate nature and the elements. He succeeded, through the power of art alone, in at least partially civilizing the unpredictable, wild and violent world, making it decorous and pleasant. He is regarded as the patron of marriage and also, curiously, of the love of boys, and as the inventor of magic. His cult spread from Thrace through the entire Greek and later Roman world, and became a veritable religion. Until the end of classical antiquity and even in the early Middle Ages, the reputation of Orpheus was so great that the early preachers of Christianity had no option but to exploit his popularity and adopt parts of his cult (for instance veneration of the good shepherd) into their own religion, associating them with Jesus – although not without emphasizing that the cult of Orpheus was primitive idolatry, that Jesus surpassed Orpheus in every respect, even as a singer whose song banished the demons and other demi-gods and minor gods forever, and that he tamed the wildest of all animals, mankind itself, leading him back to heaven. In addition, they claimed, he not only challenged but actually overcame death, both in his own person and on behalf of all humanity – he would do it at no lower a price – not to mention those whom he raised from the dead *en passant* and (unlike Orpheus) successfully. But I will allow myself to say that, whether or not they succeeded, the three resurrections performed by Jesus of Nazareth in the Biblical account cannot, in my opinion, compete with the magnificent failure of Orpheus of Thrace, either in daring or in poetic and mythological power. As an example, and evidence for my point, let us take the case of Lazarus, the most extensively described and the best known incident in which Jesus brought the dead back to life. The story goes like this:

Two ladies who are friends of Jesus send him a message saying that their brother Lazarus is sick and likely to die, and asking Jesus to come and heal him. What does Jesus do? He doesn't come. He says: "This sickness is not unto death, but for the glory of God, that the Son of God might be glorified thereby." He acts (according to St John the Evangelist, it is only fair to note), in exactly the same way as any political leader of earlier modern times and the present day when confronted by an unexpected and unwelcome event: his reflex reaction is to try turning the event to his own advantage and exploiting it for self-advertisement. The fact that a man is lying sick and suffering is of minor significance. Far more important is how to stage the saving of the invalid's life to the best effect for publicity, thus enhancing the savior's own reputation and giving his own movement a boost. Jesus does this in an extreme and indeed brutal way. He waits until Lazarus is dead, and informs his followers that he is glad that he was not there, saying it was to make them believe in him. Only now does he set off at his leisure, accompanied by his followers, to the village where Lazarus had lived, and arrives four days late. The two ladies, Mary and Martha, are understandably disappointed. "If you had been here," they say, "our brother would not have died." Jesus takes this remark as *lèse majesté*, becomes furious and shouts at the two sisters before the assembled mourners that they should not be weeping and wailing, but ought to believe in him as the Son of God, to whom nothing is impossible. Then he orders that he be taken to the grave, not without a touching performance on the way when he publicly sheds a tear, instantly achieving the desired success with his audience. "Behold how he loved him!" whispers the crowd. On reaching the grave, a kind of cavern sealed with

a stone slab, Jesus orders, "Take away the stone!" He
dismisses the objection of one of the sisters who
protests that it would be better not to, since the
dead man has been there for four days and "by this
time he stinketh." Raising his voice at her again, he
tells her to shut up and believe in him. – Sorry, that
is not an entirely correct quote, for the Messiah
expresses himself a little more elegantly. "Said I not
unto thee, that, if thou wouldest believe, thou
shouldest see the glory of God?" This is how he
speaks. Then they remove the stone. The decisive
moment has come. The crowd holds its breath. We
can picture them first staring into the dark cavern,
then looking expectantly at Jesus, we can imagine
both supporters and opponents (for there are some
of those present too) pricking up their ears, styluses
at the ready, so that not a word of the Master will
escape them and no detail will go unreported – for
John's story reads very much like a press report written after the event, and we get the impression of

attending a media spectacle of our own day. Only the TV cameras are missing.

Next comes a close-up of Jesus. Before he goes into action he creates a dramatic climax and heightens the tension with yet another delaying factor, at the same time proclaiming his own message and, with outrageous frankness, revealing the propagandist purpose of the event. He lifts up his eyes to heaven and to God, whom he addresses as his father. "Father, I thank thee that thou hast heard me. And I knew that thou hearest me always: but because of the people which stand by I said it, that they may believe that thou has sent me." Only now does he turn his eyes to the cavern and calls, with a loud voice: "Lazarus, come forth."

And the poor fellow, his head and body wrapped in a shroud, already smelling high, comes staggering out of his grave into the bright light of day and has to face the gaping crowd. "Loose him," says Jesus curtly, "and let him go."

The success of the operation is, as intended, overwhelming. The majority of the Jews present spontaneously join the Jesus party; others deploy to spread the news of his famous deed throughout the country; some go straight off to tell on him to the high priests. The high priests decide that, for their own good political reasons, they will dispose of the seditious itinerant preacher who has been a thorn in their flesh for some time by killing him. So the raising of Lazarus leads immediately to the last act in the brilliant success story of Jesus of Nazareth: his death on the cross, as foretold, desired, and instigated by himself. After that, nothing was going to stop its onward progress as propaganda.

Orpheus died in an equally cruel way. After his return from the underworld and the second, final loss of his beloved he fell into deep melancholy and abjured the pleasures of life, meaning the love of women. "Alone he would roam," as Virgil puts it, "the northern ice, the snowy Tanais, and the fields ever wedded to Rhipaean frosts, wailing Eurydice lost." This aroused the wrath of the Thracian women, possessed by Dionysian desire and wishing to be desired. Finally, when the singing youth turned them down, they stoned him to death, tore him to pieces, scattered his limbs and threw his head, nailed to his lyre, into the nearest river, where as it floated away it continued to call "with death-cold tongue, with fleeting breath, Eurydice – ah, hapless Eurydice! 'Eurydice' the banks re-echoed, all down the stream."

The life of Orpheus ends not with a well-judged "It is finished," representing the final moment of a grand plan for the salvation of the world, but with a simple lament for the one woman he loved. It began with the same lament. While the coming of Jesus as Messiah was prophesied, while he was born the Messiah and was the Messiah all his life, Orpheus entered myth and history as a man in mourning. He had lost his young wife when she was bitten by a poisonous snake. He is so inconsolable at her loss that he does something which may well appear to us mad, but is easy to understand: he wants to bring his dead beloved back to life. It is not that he questions the power of death in itself or the fact that it has the last word, still less is he concerned with overcoming death on behalf of all mankind or achieving eternal life. He wants only this one woman back, his beloved Eurydice, and he wants her back not forever and ever, just for the length of a normal human life, to be happy with her on earth. So Orpheus's venture into the underworld is not to be regarded as suicidal – he was no Werther, no Kleist, and certainly no Tristan – but as a bold venture looking towards life, and indeed desperately fighting for it. Plato, incidentally, blames him for that in the *Symposium*. Phaidros mocks the "weak musician" Orpheus, who lacked the spirit to kill himself for love and preferred to make his way into the underworld alive, as if that were child's play! For unlike Jesus, Orpheus cannot count on divine assistance in his daring exploit, although if – as many say – he was the son of Apollo he must have had good connections with Mount Olympus. On the contrary; he knowingly and willingly transgresses against divine order by making his way into the realm of the dead. Nor does he announce his deed to the whole world in advance, like his Nazarene successor, he does not make a great fuss about it, does not surround himself with disciples and onlookers so that he can stage it as a major media event, but goes alone, relying solely on himself, equipped with nothing but his lyre, his voice, and his song of lamentation. But that song – as he well knows – is beguilingly beautiful, so heart-rending that the hound of hell lies down, Charon the ferryman forgets the rules, the mollified Furies fall silent, Tantalus no longer feels his torments, Sisyphus rests from his labors for a moment, and even Persephone and Hades, the dark rulers of the world below, look at the intruder not without a certain emotion when he comes before their throne, singing.

And now he does something – or at least, so Ovid tells us – which I must admit makes him seem to me extraordinarily attractive: he makes no demands, he does not insist on his rights, he does not shout, "Come out, Eurydice!" He is not aiming to prove anything by his actions. He is unassuming and shrewd. He pleads and argues. He negotiates.

In no way, he says, does he wish to question the unbounded power of the rulers of the dead souls by intruding, uninvited, into the fields of shadow and asking them to set Eurydice free. "Yours is the longest sway over the human race" – he does not dispute that, he says, and of course Eurydice is no exception. But in her case, he pleads, the thread of life was cut far too soon, robbing the poor girl of the years allotted to her, of the bloom of her youth and her maturity. She will return to the realm of the dead sooner or later, as will he too, Orpheus, and all other mortals. So if he asks for her thread of life to be joined again, and for permission to bring his beloved back to the world above, the rulers of the underworld must take it as a request for them to cede their property, only as a loan for a limited time. After a few years or decades the woman he has borrowed back from them will return to her rightful owners forever. Moreover – and he makes much of this – he has come down to the underworld not out of calculation or curiosity or with evil intent, but solely for the sake of love. Love, he says, is a power that no earthly man can elude, and he believes that the light of love can sometimes make its way even into the deep darkness of the underworld. Was it not the power of love that once brought its rulers together? If the tales are true, did not Hades himself in his youth, driven by passionate love and ignoring an arrangement with his divine colleagues, carry

Persephone away from a flowery meadow and down to Orcus? Let the rulers remember their own youth, he pleads, their own love, and for the sake of love put mercy before justice and let Eurydice go free. If not, he too, Orpheus, will not return to the living world, but stay here among the dead.

He said all this in song.

It must be admitted that the words of Orpheus are in pleasant contrast to Jesus of Nazareth's imperious tone. Jesus was a fanatical preacher who was not trying to win his hearers over, but demanded their unconditional allegiance. His remarks are full of orders, threats, and the recurrent statement, made to clinch his case, "But I say unto you." That is how people talk when they want to love and liberate not a single person but all humanity. Orpheus, however, loves just this one woman, Eurydice, and wants to save her alone. So the tone he takes with the rulers of the underworld is more conciliatory, friendlier, pleading – he is literally wooing their favor. And lo and behold, he succeeds. The rulers of the realm of the dead give him his beloved back – though on the well-known condition that on their way home to the world above he must not turn and look back as she follows him.

And now he makes a mistake. (The Nazarene never goes wrong. Even when he does seem to make an obvious mistake – admitting a traitor into his own close circle, for instance – it is deliberate and part of the plan of salvation.) Orpheus, however, is a man without superhuman aims and abilities, and as such it is always possible for him to make a bad mistake, do something appallingly stupid – which again makes him likeable. He is happy, and who can blame him? He is overjoyed at his success. After all, he has done something that no one has ever done before: he has brought his beloved back from the dead, back to life. Almost. It's as good as done. The short way that still lies before him holds no dangers, he thinks. No hound of hell lurks there, no Erinnyes, and what is more he – or rather they, he and the companion walking behind him – are travelling by permission of the highest powers. So what could go wrong? The cause is won, his triumph is complete. So he thinks. And in the exuberance of his happiness he begins to sing again, not a lament now, of course, but a jubilant hymn to life, to love, to Eurydice. The beauty of his own singing enraptures him so much that he underestimates the danger still threatening his venture, perhaps no longer even sees it – for that danger comes from within himself.

Orpheus, we must remember, is an artist, and like all artists not without vanity, or let us say not without pride in his art. And like many artists, particularly in the performing arts, he relies on an audience to watch him, listen to him, applaud him or at least react to him in some way, an audience from whose behavior he can assess the effect of his singing. When he climbed down into the underworld, that effect was obvious. "The pale souls wept" with emotion, as Ovid writes, and not just the rulers of that realm but also the many nameless dead. All who heard him were at his feet – he must have had an audience of millions. But now, climbing up again through rugged, difficult terrain, too far from the dead and not yet close enough to the living, no one was listening to him any more. Except the one walking behind him. And she has said nothing. Why not? Had she been forbidden to speak? Couldn't she even call out, "Bravo!" or "Beautiful!" Couldn't she at least clap her hands in joy and rapture? Was she still there at all? Had she lost contact with him somewhere along the way? Or had she perhaps never been behind him at all? Was it possible – and he thought that terrible thought even as he went on singing, for naturally he was a highly neurotic, which is to say a perfectly normal man – was it possible that he had been tricked all along just to get rid of him, since he was not to be shaken off in any other way, and his beloved had never been following him? Was that childish condition, that pointless ban on turning round imposed only so that he wouldn't notice the ruse, or notice only when it was too late to turn back? And perhaps he had been fool enough to fall for it, and was walking, singing happily like an idiot, all alone through the deserted wilderness . . . ! He was still singing, and sang louder than ever, in rage and rising despair, to get himself a hearing, not knowing from whom: Eurydice, he sang, Eurydice . . . !

No opera singer can go on performing with his back to the audience for very long . . . even if the director asks him to do it a thousand times, either threatening him or speaking with the tongues of angels. He can't do it. It is against his nature. His whole art and *raison d'être* consists in turning his own soul inside out, and he *must* show himself off, *must* turn to himself to see the reflection of his soul. And a moment will come, in spite of all prohibitions, when he docs.

Orpheus, suffering the double torment of being unable to turn to himself and thinking that he had perhaps been cheated from the first, held out for an astonishingly long time. He was "on the very verge of light," writes Virgil, already on safe ground himself, back in this world, when his self-control cracked. Presumably he no longer expected to see her behind him. He could have lived with divine fraud, he could have taken refuge in thoughts of rage and revenge. But now that he turned round, he saw to his surprise and indeed horror that she really was there, not two paces away but still on the wrong side of the border, and he lost her through his own fault. She looked at him, as horrified as he was, and with endless melancholy but no reproach breathed a barely audible "Farewell," and sank back into the underworld forever.

THE STORY OF ORPHEUS MOVES US TO THIS DAY because it is a story of failure. That wonderful attempt to reconcile the two mysterious and primeval forces of human existence, love and death, and move the fiercer of the two to come to at least a small compromise, failed in the end. The story of Jesus, on the other hand, was triumphant from the beginning to the bitter end in his confrontation with death. Only twice did he show human weakness: in Gethsemane, when he briefly doubted his mission ("If it be possible, let this cup pass from me") and then in shattering clarity on the cross, with his entirely unexpected last words, "My God, my God, why has thou forsaken me?", which were not part of the plan. This cry of despair, however, is recorded only in the first two Gospels. In Luke and John, written later, it does not feature, probably being seen as politically incorrect, and was replaced by the self-confident, "Father, into thy hands I commend my spirit!", or as quoted above from John, "It is finished!"

And what about love? That sensuously demanding, urgent Eros of which we spoke? Not a chance. Eros meant nothing to Jesus. The Devil knew that when he led him into temptation. Unlimited pretty girls or catamites were not the kind of bait to catch that sour young carpenter. All that interested him was *power*. And so the Devil offered him power over "all the kingdoms of the world, and the glory of them" if he would fall down and worship him – in vain, as we know, for while Jesus had no intention of renouncing power he was relying on the other, stronger party in the contest to help him get it.

This calculating aspect of his nature, his almost unremitting self-control, his immunity to the frenzy of Eros lends a chill to the person of Jesus of Nazareth, a sense of distance and inhumanity. But perhaps we ask too much of him. Perhaps he really was only a god.

Orpheus is closer to us there. In spite of his emotional extravagance and later waywardness, he is closer to us in his straightforward courage, his civilized attitude, his entirely spontaneous wit and shrewdness, and that both despite and because of his failure, Orpheus was undoubtedly the more complete human being.